MULTIPLICATION AND DIVISION

MATH WORKBOOK

Scholastic Panda
Education

Check Out Our Other Books

ISBN: 978-1953149060

Copyright © 2020 by Scholastic Panda Education
Second Paperback Edition: June 2020
First Paperback Edition: April 2019

MULTIPLICATION TABLE

X	0	1	2	3	4	5	6	7	8	9	10	11	12
0	0	0	0	0	0	0	0	0	0	0	0	0	0
1	0	1	2	3	4	5	6	7	8	9	10	11	12
2	0	2	4	6	8	10	12	14	16	18	20	22	24
3	0	3	6	9	12	15	18	21	24	27	30	33	36
4	0	4	8	12	16	20	24	28	32	36	40	44	48
5	0	5	10	15	20	25	30	35	40	45	50	55	60
6	0	6	12	18	24	30	36	42	48	54	60	66	72
7	0	7	14	21	28	35	42	49	56	63	70	77	84
8	0	8	16	24	32	40	48	56	64	72	80	88	96
9	0	9	18	27	36	45	54	63	72	81	90	99	108
10	0	10	20	30	40	50	60	70	80	90	100	110	120
11	0	11	22	33	44	55	66	77	88	99	110	121	132
12	0	12	24	36	48	60	72	84	96	108	120	132	144

MULTIPLICATION BASICS

Factors

7 x 3 = 21

factors

Product

7 x 3 = 21

product

Times

7 x 3 = 21

times

Multiplication Sentence

7 x 3 = 21

7 times 3 equals 21

Communicative Property

7 x 3 = 21

3 x 7 = 21

Numbers can be multiplied in any order. The result remains the same.

Arrays

△ △ △ △ △
△ △ △ △ △
△ △ △ △ △

A set of objects arranged in equal rows and columns.

MULTIPLYING BY ONE-DIGIT NUMBERS

When multiplying, you must multiply one place at a time.

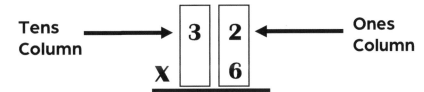

Tens Column → | 3 | 2 | ← Ones Column

```
    3   2
  x     6
```

```
   32
 x  6
```
Multiply 6 ones x 2 ones to get 12 ones.

```
    1
   32
 x  6
    2
```
Place 1 ten in the tens column above the 3 tens.

Regroup because 12 ones = 1 ten and 2 ones.

Place 2 ones in the ones column.

```
    1
   32
 x  6
  192
```
Multiply 6 ones x 3 tens to get 18 tens.

Add the 1 ten to the 18 tens to get 19 tens.

Place 19 tens below.

Below are more examples:

```
   2          3          1          2         4 3        2 4 2
  64         39         72         98        254        4,374
x  7       x  4       x  8       x  3       x  9        x   6
  44         15         57         29       2,286       26,244
   8          6          6          4
```

MULTIPLYING BY TWO-DIGIT NUMBERS

To multiply by two-digit numbers, you must first multiply by the ones digit, and then by the tens digit.

```
  1 1
  432
x  76
─────
2,592
```

1) Multiply each digit of the first factor by 6 ones.

2) Regroup as needed.

2,592 ← **This is a partial product.**   **432 x 6 = 2,592**

```
  2 1
  432
x  76
─────
2,592
30,240
```

3) Multiply each digit of the first factor by 7 tens.

4) Write this number under the partial product found in step 1.

5) Regroup as needed.

30,240 ← **This is also partial product.**   **432 x 70 = 30,240**

(Notice the 0 as a placeholder, which can be left out.)

```
   432
 x  76
──────
 2,592
30,240
──────
32,832
```

6) Add the partial products: 2,592 + 30,240 = 32,832

Below are more examples:

```
    39          72          52          254        4,374
 x  34       x  98       x  43       x   29       x   76
 ──────      ──────      ──────      ───────      ───────
    156         576         156        2,286       26,244
   1170       6,480       2,080        5,080      306,180
 ──────      ──────      ──────      ───────      ───────
   1326       7,056       2,236        7,366      332,424
```

MULTIPLYING BY 10, 100 or 1,000

– THE LONG WAY –

- To multiply by 10, 100 or 1,000, simply multiply the digits one place at a time

$$\begin{array}{r} 32 \\ \times\ 10 \\ \hline 320 \end{array}$$

Multiply 0 x 2 ones to get 0.

Multiply 1 ten x 2 ones to get 2 tens or 20.

Multiply 1 ten x 3 ones to get 3 tens or 30.

– THE FASTER WAY –

- To multiply any whole number by <u>10</u>, write the whole number and then place a zero (0) to the end of it.

$$\begin{array}{r} 72 \\ \times\ 10 \\ \hline 720 \end{array}$$

The whole number is 72. Place a 0 at the end to make it 720. Easy, right?

- To multiply any whole number by <u>100</u>, write the whole number and then place two zeros (00) to the end of it.

$$\begin{array}{r} 832 \\ \times\ 100 \\ \hline 83,200 \end{array}$$

- To multiply any whole number by <u>1000</u>, write the whole number and then place three zeros (000) to the end of it.

$$\begin{array}{r} 549 \\ \times\ 1000 \\ \hline 549,00 \\ 0 \end{array}$$

The whole number is 549. Place three zeros at the end to make it 549,000.

You can continue repeat this process four zeros for 10,000 and so on. Give it a try!

MULTIPLYING BY TWO-, THREE-, AND FOUR-DIGIT NUMBERS

To multiply large numbers, you have to multiply one place at a time.

$$
\begin{array}{r}
^{2\ 1} \\
232 \\
\times\ 587 \\
\hline
1,624
\end{array}
$$

1) Multiply each digit of the first factor by 7 ones.

2) Regroup as needed.

1,624 ← **Partial product.** 232 x 7 = 1,624

$$
\begin{array}{r}
^{2\ 1} \\
232 \\
\times\ 587 \\
\hline
1,624 \\
18,560
\end{array}
$$

3) Multiply each digit of the first factor by 8 tens.

4) Write this number under the partial product found in step 1.

5) Regroup as needed.

18,560 ← **Partial product.** 232 x 80 = 18,560
(Notice the 0 as a placeholder, which can be left out.)

$$
\begin{array}{r}
232 \\
\times\ 587 \\
\hline
1,624 \\
18,560 \\
116,000
\end{array}
$$

6) Multiply each digit of the first factor by 5 hundreds.

7) Regroup as needed.

8) 232 x 500 = 116,000

9) Line up the partial products, making sure they're in the proper place.

136,184   **10)** Add the partial products: **1,624 + 18,560 + 116,000 = 136,184**

....

Below are more examples:

$\begin{array}{r}939\\\times\ 234\end{array}$	$\begin{array}{r}362\\\times\ 123\end{array}$	$\begin{array}{r}321\\\times\ 581\end{array}$	$\begin{array}{r}441\\\times\ 144\end{array}$
3,756	1,086	321	1,764
28,170	7,240	25,680	17,640
187,800	36,200	160,500	44,100
219,726	**44,526**	**186,501**	**63,504**

THE BOX METHOD

Another way to multiply large numbers is to break them down into place value parts, making them easier to manage

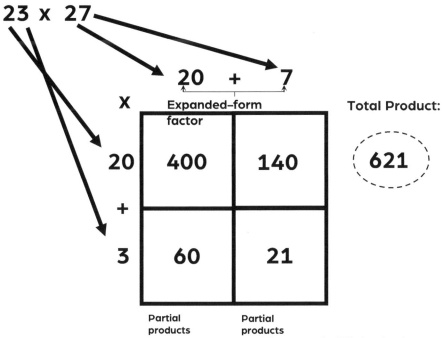

1) Determine how many boxes you will need. This is based on the number of digits you're multiplying.

2) 23 is two digits, 20 in the tens place and 3 in the ones place. Therefore, you'll need two boxes down.

3) 27 is two digits, 20 in the tens place and 7 in the ones place. Therefore, you'll need two boxes across.

4) Multiply each digit on the outside of the box and fill the answer in the appropriate box inside.

$$20 \times 20 = 400$$
$$20 \times 7 = 140$$
$$3 \times 20 = 60$$
$$3 \times 7 = 21$$

5) Add all of the numbers inside the boxes to get the total product.
400 + 140 + 60 + 21 = 621

BOX METHOD EXAMPLES

Another way to multiply large numbers is to break them down into place value parts, making them easier to manage

12 x 412

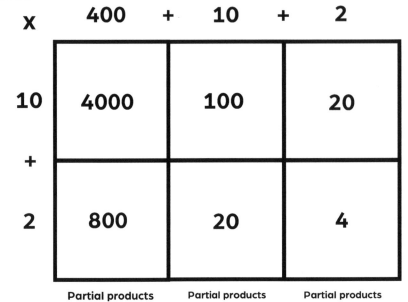

x	400 +	10 +	2
10	4000	100	20
+ 2	800	20	4
	Partial products	Partial products	Partial products

Total Product:

4,944

37 x 681

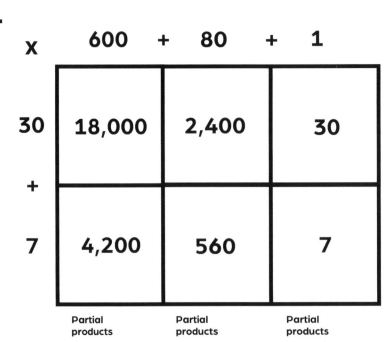

x	600 +	80 +	1
30	18,000	2,400	30
+ 7	4,200	560	7
	Partial products	Partial products	Partial products

Total Product:

25,197

EXERCISE 1

WRITE THE MULTIPLACTION SENTENCE FOR EACH ADDITION SENTENCE

1 | 4+4+4+4+4+4   _____ X _____ = _____

2 | 7+7+7   _____ X _____ = _____

3 | 3+3+3+3+3   _____ X _____ = _____

4 | 6+6   _____ X _____ = _____

5 | 2+2+2+2+2+2+2   _____ X _____ = _____

6 | 8+8+8+8+8+8+8+8   _____ X _____ = _____

7 | 1+1+1+1+1   _____ X _____ = _____

8 | 10+10+10+10   _____ X _____ = _____

9 | 5+5+5+5+5+5+5+5+5   _____ X _____ = _____

10 | 9+9+9+9+9   _____ X _____ = _____

EXERCISE 2

WRITE THE MULTIPLACTION SENTENCE FOR EACH ADDITION SENTENCE

1   9+9+9+9   _____ X _____ = _____

2   2+2+2+2+2   _____ X _____ = _____

3   8+8+8+8+8   _____ X _____ = _____

4   3+3   _____ X _____ = _____

5   12+12+12+12+12+12   _____ X _____ = _____

6   5+5+5+5+5+5+5   _____ X _____ = _____

7   4+4+4+4   _____ X _____ = _____

8   11+11+11+11+11   _____ X _____ = _____

9   1+1+1+1+1+1+1+1   _____ X _____ = _____

10   14+14+14+14+14   _____ X _____ = _____

EXERCISE 3

COMMUNICATIVE PROPERTY OF MULTIPLICATION

1 If 4 x 3 = 12, then 3 x 4=

2 If 8 x 7 = 56, then 7 x 8=

3 If 2 x 12 = 24, then 12 x 2=

4 If 5 x 9 = 45, then 9 x 5=

5 If 6 x 8 = 48, then 8 x 6 =

Fill in the blanks

9 x 3 = 3 x _____   _____ x _____ = 3 x 5

7 x 6 = 6 x _____   4 x 1 = 1 x _____

4 x 8 = _____ x 8   _____ x 7 = 7 x 2

_____ x 5 = 5 x 10   _____ x _____ = 5 x 8

_____ x _____ = 2 x 12   10 x 4 = 4 x _____

EXERCISE 4

1	How many bathtubs are there?	_____
2	How many fish are in one bathtub?	_____
3	How many total fish are there?	____ X ____ = ____

1	How many bags are there?	_____
2	How many apples are in each bag?	_____
3	How many total apples are there?	____ X ____ = ____

EXERCISE 5

| 1 | How many boxes are there? | _____ |

| 2 | How many butterflies are in each box? | _____ |

| 3 | How many total butterflies are there? | _____ X _____ = _____ |

| 1 | How many squares are there? | _____ |

| 2 | How many diamonds are in one square? | _____ |

| 3 | How many total diamonds are there? | _____ X _____ = _____ |

EXERCISE 6

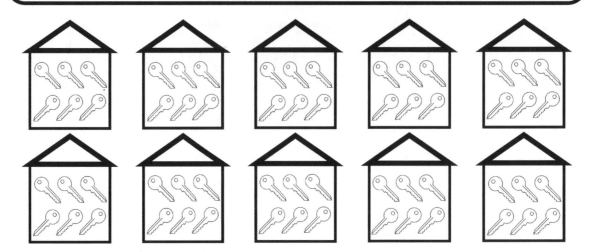

1	How many houses are there?	_____
2	How many keys are in each house?	_____
3	How many total keys are there?	_____ X _____ = _____

1	How many squares are there?	_____
2	How many gears are in each square?	_____
3	How many total gears are there?	_____ X _____ = _____

EXERCISE 7

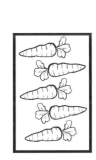  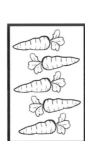 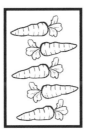  

1	How many rectangles are there?	_____
2	How many carrots are in each rectangle?	_____
3	How many total carrots are there?	____ X ____ = ____

1	How many cages are there?	_____
2	How many birds are in each cage?	_____
3	How many total birds are there?	____ X ____ = ____

EXERCISE 8

WRITE THE MULTIPLACTION SENTENCE FOR EACH ARRAY

1

△ △ △ △ △
△ △ △ △ △
△ △ △ △ △

_____ ✕ _____ = _____

2

△ △ △
△ △ △
△ △ △

_____ ✕ _____ = _____

3

△ △ △ △
△ △ △ △
△ △ △ △

_____ ✕ _____ = _____

4

△ △ △ △ △ △ △

_____ ✕ _____ = _____

5

△ △ △ △ △ △ △
△ △ △ △ △ △ △
△ △ △ △ △ △ △

_____ ✕ _____ = _____

6

△ △ △ △ △ △ △
△ △ △ △ △ △ △

_____ ✕ _____ = _____

7

△ △
△ △
△ △
△ △

_____ ✕ _____ = _____

8

△ △
△ △

_____ ✕ _____ = _____

EXERCISE 9

WRITE THE MULTIPLACTION SENTENCE FOR EACH ARRAY

1

☆ ☆ ☆
☆ ☆ ☆
☆ ☆ ☆

_____ X _____ = _____

2

☆ ☆ ☆ ☆ ☆ ☆ ☆ ☆
☆ ☆ ☆ ☆ ☆ ☆ ☆ ☆

_____ X _____ = _____

3

☆ ☆
☆ ☆
☆ ☆
☆ ☆
☆ ☆

_____ X _____ = _____

4

☆ ☆ ☆ ☆ ☆ ☆

_____ X _____ = _____

5

☆ ☆ ☆ ☆ ☆
☆ ☆ ☆ ☆ ☆
☆ ☆ ☆ ☆ ☆

_____ X _____ = _____

6

☆ ☆ ☆ ☆
☆ ☆ ☆ ☆

_____ X _____ = _____

7

☆ ☆
☆ ☆
☆ ☆

_____ X _____ = _____

8

☆ ☆ ☆ ☆ ☆ ☆ ☆ ☆ ☆
☆ ☆ ☆ ☆ ☆ ☆ ☆ ☆ ☆
☆ ☆ ☆ ☆ ☆ ☆ ☆ ☆ ☆

_____ X _____ = _____

EXERCISE 10

COLOR IN EACH ARRAY FOR THE MULTIPLICATION EQUATIONS BELOW

2 x 4 = 8

1

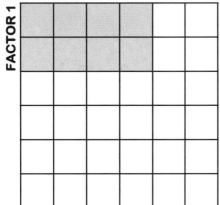

1 x 2 = 2

2

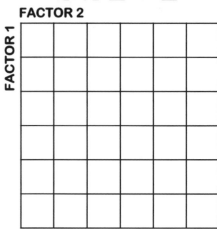

6 x 3 = 18

3

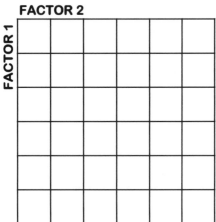

5 x 6 = 30

4

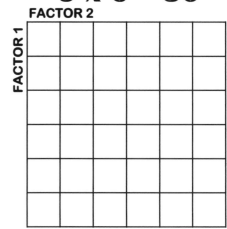

3 x 4 = 12

5

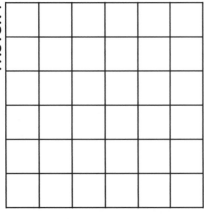

4 x 4 = 16

6

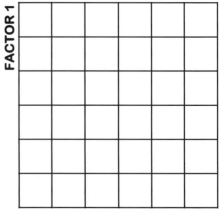

EXERCISE 11

COLOR IN EACH ARRAY FOR THE MULTIPLICATION EQUATIONS BELOW

1

6 x 2 = 12

FACTOR 2

FACTOR 1

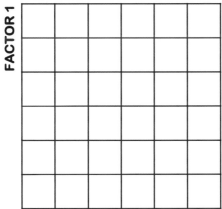

2

3 x 2 = 6

FACTOR 2

FACTOR 1

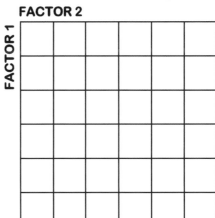

3

5 x 3 = 15

FACTOR 2

FACTOR 1

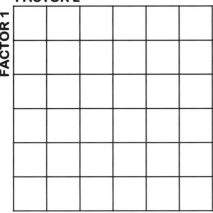

4

2 x 2 = 4

FACTOR 2

FACTOR 1

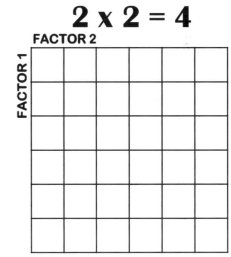

5

3 x 3 = 9

FACTOR 2

FACTOR 1

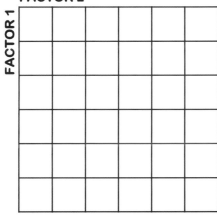

6

5 x 1 = 5

FACTOR 2

FACTOR 1

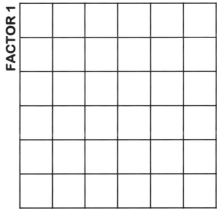

EXERCISE 12

DRAW AN ARRAY FOR THE MULTIPLICATION EQUATIONS BELOW

$5 \times 7 = 35$

1

FACTOR 2

FACTOR 1

$6 \times 1 = 6$

2

FACTOR 2

FACTOR 1

$8 \times 2 = 16$

3

FACTOR 2

FACTOR 1

$5 \times 9 = 45$

4

FACTOR 2

FACTOR 1

$4 \times 3 = 12$

5

FACTOR 2

FACTOR 1

$2 \times 9 = 18$

6

FACTOR 2

FACTOR 1

EXERCISE 13

DRAW AN ARRAY FOR THE MULTIPLICATION EQUATIONS BELOW

$8 \times 8 = 64$

1   FACTOR 2

FACTOR 1

$9 \times 4 = 36$

2   FACTOR 2

FACTOR 1

$4 \times 10 = 40$

3   FACTOR 2

FACTOR 1

$6 \times 9 = 54$

4   FACTOR 2

FACTOR 1

$2 \times 12 = 24$

5   FACTOR 2

FACTOR 1

$9 \times 1 = 9$

6   FACTOR 2

FACTOR 1

EXERCISE 14

MULTIPLY BY 2

X	0	1	2	3	4	5	6	7	8	9	10	11	12
2													

$$
\begin{array}{r} 8 \\ \times\ 2 \\ \hline \end{array}
\qquad
\begin{array}{r} 3 \\ \times\ 2 \\ \hline \end{array}
\qquad
\begin{array}{r} 12 \\ \times\ 2 \\ \hline \end{array}
\qquad
\begin{array}{r} 2 \\ \times\ 13 \\ \hline \end{array}
\qquad
\begin{array}{r} 7 \\ \times\ 2 \\ \hline \end{array}
$$

$$
\begin{array}{r} 2 \\ \times\ 11 \\ \hline \end{array}
\qquad
\begin{array}{r} 2 \\ \times\ 16 \\ \hline \end{array}
\qquad
\begin{array}{r} 9 \\ \times\ 2 \\ \hline \end{array}
\qquad
\begin{array}{r} 2 \\ \times\ 6 \\ \hline \end{array}
\qquad
\begin{array}{r} 2 \\ \times\ 5 \\ \hline \end{array}
$$

$$
\begin{array}{r} 4 \\ \times\ 2 \\ \hline \end{array}
\qquad
\begin{array}{r} 2 \\ \times\ 1 \\ \hline \end{array}
\qquad
\begin{array}{r} 0 \\ \times\ 2 \\ \hline \end{array}
\qquad
\begin{array}{r} 6 \\ \times\ 2 \\ \hline \end{array}
\qquad
\begin{array}{r} 2 \\ \times\ 5 \\ \hline \end{array}
$$

$2 \times 9 =$ _____ $5 \times 2 =$ _____ $2 \times 2 =$ _____

$2 \times 5 =$ _____ $2 \times 11 =$ _____ $2 \times 4 =$ _____

$7 \times 2 =$ _____ $2 \times 8 =$ _____ $13 \times 2 =$ _____

$2 \times 6 =$ _____ $2 \times 12 =$ _____ $8 \times 2 =$ _____

EXERCISE 15

MULTIPLY BY 3

X	0	1	2	3	4	5	6	7	8	9	10	11	12
3													

$$
\begin{array}{ccccc}
8 & 3 & 12 & 3 & 7 \\
\times\ 3 & \times\ 3 & \times\ 3 & \times\ 1 & \times\ 3 \\
\end{array}
$$

$$
\begin{array}{ccccc}
3 & 3 & 9 & 0 & 3 \\
\times\ 11 & \times\ 6 & \times\ 3 & \times\ 3 & \times\ 5 \\
\end{array}
$$

$$
\begin{array}{ccccc}
4 & 3 & 1 & 6 & 3 \\
\times\ 3 & \times\ 9 & \times\ 3 & \times\ 3 & \times\ 5 \\
\end{array}
$$

$9 \times 3 =$ _____ $3 \times 5 =$ _____ $3 \times 3 =$ _____

$5 \times 3 =$ _____ $11 \times 3 =$ _____ $4 \times 3 =$ _____

$3 \times 7 =$ _____ $8 \times 3 =$ _____ $3 \times 10 =$ _____

$6 \times 3 =$ _____ $12 \times 3 =$ _____ $3 \times 2 =$ _____

EXERCISE 16

MULTIPLY BY 4

X	0	1	2	3	4	5	6	7	8	9	10	11	12
4													

$$\begin{array}{r} 4 \\ \times\ 8 \\ \hline \end{array} \qquad \begin{array}{r} 0 \\ \times\ 4 \\ \hline \end{array} \qquad \begin{array}{r} 4 \\ \times\ 12 \\ \hline \end{array} \qquad \begin{array}{r} 13 \\ \times\ 4 \\ \hline \end{array} \qquad \begin{array}{r} 4 \\ \times\ 7 \\ \hline \end{array}$$

$$\begin{array}{r} 11 \\ \times\ 4 \\ \hline \end{array} \qquad \begin{array}{r} 16 \\ \times\ 4 \\ \hline \end{array} \qquad \begin{array}{r} 4 \\ \times\ 9 \\ \hline \end{array} \qquad \begin{array}{r} 4 \\ \times\ 1 \\ \hline \end{array} \qquad \begin{array}{r} 5 \\ \times\ 4 \\ \hline \end{array}$$

$$\begin{array}{r} 3 \\ \times\ 4 \\ \hline \end{array} \qquad \begin{array}{r} 9 \\ \times\ 4 \\ \hline \end{array} \qquad \begin{array}{r} 4 \\ \times\ 4 \\ \hline \end{array} \qquad \begin{array}{r} 4 \\ \times\ 6 \\ \hline \end{array} \qquad \begin{array}{r} 4 \\ \times\ 10 \\ \hline \end{array}$$

4 x 9 = _____   3 x 4 = _____   4 x 5 = _____

4 x 3 = _____   4 x 11 = _____   4 x 4 = _____

7 x 4 = _____   4 x 8 = _____   10 x 4 = _____

8 x 4 = _____   0 x 4 = _____   2 x 4 = _____

EXERCISE 17

MULTIPLY BY 5

X	0	1	2	3	4	5	6	7	8	9	10	11	12
5													

$$
\begin{array}{r} 8 \\ \times\ 5 \\ \hline \end{array}
\qquad
\begin{array}{r} 5 \\ \times\ 5 \\ \hline \end{array}
\qquad
\begin{array}{r} 1 \\ \times\ 5 \\ \hline \end{array}
\qquad
\begin{array}{r} 5 \\ \times\ 0 \\ \hline \end{array}
\qquad
\begin{array}{r} 7 \\ \times\ 5 \\ \hline \end{array}
$$

$$
\begin{array}{r} 5 \\ \times\ 11 \\ \hline \end{array}
\qquad
\begin{array}{r} 6 \\ \times\ 5 \\ \hline \end{array}
\qquad
\begin{array}{r} 9 \\ \times\ 5 \\ \hline \end{array}
\qquad
\begin{array}{r} 5 \\ \times\ 1 \\ \hline \end{array}
\qquad
\begin{array}{r} 4 \\ \times\ 5 \\ \hline \end{array}
$$

$$
\begin{array}{r} 5 \\ \times\ 3 \\ \hline \end{array}
\qquad
\begin{array}{r} 5 \\ \times\ 9 \\ \hline \end{array}
\qquad
\begin{array}{r} 5 \\ \times\ 5 \\ \hline \end{array}
\qquad
\begin{array}{r} 5 \\ \times\ 6 \\ \hline \end{array}
\qquad
\begin{array}{r} 10 \\ \times\ 5 \\ \hline \end{array}
$$

5 x 5 = _____   5 x 3 = _____   5 x 4 = _____

3 x 5 = _____   1 x 5 = _____   5 x 5 = _____

5 x 7 = _____   8 x 5 = _____   5 x 10 = _____

5 x 8 = _____   5 x 0 = _____   5 x 2 = _____

EXERCISE 18

MULTIPLY BY 6

X	0	1	2	3	4	5	6	7	8	9	10	11	12
6													

$$\begin{array}{r} 6 \\ \times\ 8 \\ \hline \end{array} \qquad \begin{array}{r} 6 \\ \times\ 1 \\ \hline \end{array} \qquad \begin{array}{r} 1 \\ \times\ 6 \\ \hline \end{array} \qquad \begin{array}{r} 0 \\ \times\ 6 \\ \hline \end{array} \qquad \begin{array}{r} 6 \\ \times\ 7 \\ \hline \end{array}$$

$$\begin{array}{r} 11 \\ \times\ 6 \\ \hline \end{array} \qquad \begin{array}{r} 6 \\ \times\ 5 \\ \hline \end{array} \qquad \begin{array}{r} 6 \\ \times\ 9 \\ \hline \end{array} \qquad \begin{array}{r} 6 \\ \times\ 6 \\ \hline \end{array} \qquad \begin{array}{r} 6 \\ \times\ 4 \\ \hline \end{array}$$

$$\begin{array}{r} 3 \\ \times\ 6 \\ \hline \end{array} \qquad \begin{array}{r} 9 \\ \times\ 6 \\ \hline \end{array} \qquad \begin{array}{r} 6 \\ \times\ 2 \\ \hline \end{array} \qquad \begin{array}{r} 5 \\ \times\ 6 \\ \hline \end{array} \qquad \begin{array}{r} 6 \\ \times\ 10 \\ \hline \end{array}$$

6 x 6 = _____   6 x 7 = _____   5 x 6 = _____

3 x 6 = _____   6 x 11 = _____   12 x 6 = _____

7 x 6 = _____   6 x 8 = _____   10 x 6 = _____

8 x 6 = _____   0 x 6 = _____   2 x 6 = _____

EXERCISE 19

MULTIPLY BY 7

X	0	1	2	3	4	5	6	7	8	9	10	11	12
7													

$$\begin{array}{r} 8 \\ \times\ 7 \\ \hline \end{array} \qquad \begin{array}{r} 1 \\ \times\ 7 \\ \hline \end{array} \qquad \begin{array}{r} 7 \\ \times\ 1 \\ \hline \end{array} \qquad \begin{array}{r} 7 \\ \times\ 0 \\ \hline \end{array} \qquad \begin{array}{r} 7 \\ \times\ 6 \\ \hline \end{array}$$

$$\begin{array}{r} 7 \\ \times\ 11 \\ \hline \end{array} \qquad \begin{array}{r} 5 \\ \times\ 7 \\ \hline \end{array} \qquad \begin{array}{r} 9 \\ \times\ 7 \\ \hline \end{array} \qquad \begin{array}{r} 7 \\ \times\ 3 \\ \hline \end{array} \qquad \begin{array}{r} 4 \\ \times\ 7 \\ \hline \end{array}$$

$$\begin{array}{r} 0 \\ \times\ 7 \\ \hline \end{array} \qquad \begin{array}{r} 7 \\ \times\ 9 \\ \hline \end{array} \qquad \begin{array}{r} 2 \\ \times\ 7 \\ \hline \end{array} \qquad \begin{array}{r} 7 \\ \times\ 6 \\ \hline \end{array} \qquad \begin{array}{r} 10 \\ \times\ 7 \\ \hline \end{array}$$

7 x 7 = _____   7 x 6 = _____   7 x 5 = _____

7 x 3 = _____   11 x 7 = _____   7 x 12 = _____

6 x 7 = _____   8 x 7 = _____   7 x 10 = _____

7 x 8 = _____   7 x 0 = _____   7 x 2 = _____

EXERCISE 20

MULTIPLY BY 8

X	0	1	2	3	4	5	6	7	8	9	10	11	12
8													

$$\begin{array}{r} 7 \\ \times\ 8 \\ \hline \end{array} \qquad \begin{array}{r} 8 \\ \times\ 1 \\ \hline \end{array} \qquad \begin{array}{r} 1 \\ \times\ 8 \\ \hline \end{array} \qquad \begin{array}{r} 0 \\ \times\ 8 \\ \hline \end{array} \qquad \begin{array}{r} 3 \\ \times\ 8 \\ \hline \end{array}$$

$$\begin{array}{r} 8 \\ \times\ 8 \\ \hline \end{array} \qquad \begin{array}{r} 8 \\ \times\ 7 \\ \hline \end{array} \qquad \begin{array}{r} 8 \\ \times\ 9 \\ \hline \end{array} \qquad \begin{array}{r} 3 \\ \times\ 8 \\ \hline \end{array} \qquad \begin{array}{r} 8 \\ \times\ 4 \\ \hline \end{array}$$

$$\begin{array}{r} 8 \\ \times\ 11 \\ \hline \end{array} \qquad \begin{array}{r} 9 \\ \times\ 8 \\ \hline \end{array} \qquad \begin{array}{r} 8 \\ \times\ 2 \\ \hline \end{array} \qquad \begin{array}{r} 6 \\ \times\ 8 \\ \hline \end{array} \qquad \begin{array}{r} 8 \\ \times\ 0 \\ \hline \end{array}$$

8 x 12 = _____   6 x 8 = _____   5 x 8 = _____

3 x 8 = _____   8 x 11 = _____   1 x 8 = _____

8 x 6 = _____   8 x 3 = _____   0 x 8 = _____

8 x 7 = _____   8 x 9 = _____   2 x 8 = _____

EXERCISE 21

MULTIPLY BY 9

X	0	1	2	3	4	5	6	7	8	9	10	11	12
9													

$$\begin{array}{r} 9 \\ \times\ 7 \\ \hline \end{array} \qquad \begin{array}{r} 1 \\ \times\ 9 \\ \hline \end{array} \qquad \begin{array}{r} 9 \\ \times\ 0 \\ \hline \end{array} \qquad \begin{array}{r} 9 \\ \times\ 2 \\ \hline \end{array} \qquad \begin{array}{r} 9 \\ \times\ 3 \\ \hline \end{array}$$

$$\begin{array}{r} 11 \\ \times\ 9 \\ \hline \end{array} \qquad \begin{array}{r} 7 \\ \times\ 9 \\ \hline \end{array} \qquad \begin{array}{r} 9 \\ \times\ 9 \\ \hline \end{array} \qquad \begin{array}{r} 9 \\ \times\ 10 \\ \hline \end{array} \qquad \begin{array}{r} 4 \\ \times\ 9 \\ \hline \end{array}$$

$$\begin{array}{r} 2 \\ \times\ 9 \\ \hline \end{array} \qquad \begin{array}{r} 8 \\ \times\ 9 \\ \hline \end{array} \qquad \begin{array}{r} 3 \\ \times\ 9 \\ \hline \end{array} \qquad \begin{array}{r} 9 \\ \times\ 8 \\ \hline \end{array} \qquad \begin{array}{r} 0 \\ \times\ 9 \\ \hline \end{array}$$

12 x 9 = _____   9 x 6 = _____   9 x 5 = _____

9 x 3 = _____   11 x 9 = _____   1 x 9 = _____

4 x 9 = _____   3 x 9 = _____   9 x 0 = _____

7 x 9 = _____   9 x 8 = _____   9 x 12 = _____

EXERCISE 22

MULTIPLY BY 10

X	0	1	2	3	4	5	6	7	8	9	10	11	12
10													

```
    7          10           0           2           3
 x 10        x   1        x 10        x 10        x 10
_____     _____      _____     _____     _____


    9          10          10          10          10
 x 10        x   7        x 10        x   9        x   4
_____     _____      _____     _____     _____


   10          10          10           8          11
 x   2        x   8        x   3       x 10        x 10
_____     _____      _____     _____     _____
```

1 x 10 = _____   6 x 10 = _____   12 x 10 = _____

2 x 10 = _____   11 x 10 = _____   7 x 10 = _____

10 x 4 = _____   10 x 8 = _____   10 x 0 = _____

10 x 7 = _____   5 x 10 = _____   9 x 10 = _____

EXERCISE 23

MULTIPLY BY 11

X	0	1	2	3	4	5	6	7	8	9	10	11	12
11													

$$\begin{array}{r} 11 \\ \times\ 7 \\ \hline \end{array} \qquad \begin{array}{r} 11 \\ \times\ 1 \\ \hline \end{array} \qquad \begin{array}{r} 11 \\ \times\ 10 \\ \hline \end{array} \qquad \begin{array}{r} 11 \\ \times\ 2 \\ \hline \end{array} \qquad \begin{array}{r} 11 \\ \times\ 3 \\ \hline \end{array}$$

$$\begin{array}{r} 11 \\ \times\ 9 \\ \hline \end{array} \qquad \begin{array}{r} 0 \\ \times\ 11 \\ \hline \end{array} \qquad \begin{array}{r} 11 \\ \times\ 11 \\ \hline \end{array} \qquad \begin{array}{r} 9 \\ \times\ 11 \\ \hline \end{array} \qquad \begin{array}{r} 4 \\ \times\ 11 \\ \hline \end{array}$$

$$\begin{array}{r} 2 \\ \times\ 11 \\ \hline \end{array} \qquad \begin{array}{r} 11 \\ \times\ 8 \\ \hline \end{array} \qquad \begin{array}{r} 3 \\ \times\ 11 \\ \hline \end{array} \qquad \begin{array}{r} 11 \\ \times\ 6 \\ \hline \end{array} \qquad \begin{array}{r} 11 \\ \times\ 5 \\ \hline \end{array}$$

11 x 1 = _____   11 x 2 = _____   11 x 12 = _____

11 x 9 = _____   11 x 10 = _____   11 x 7 = _____

4 x 11 = _____   8 x 11 = _____   0 x 11 = _____

7 x 11 = _____   11 x 5 = _____   3 x 11 = _____

EXERCISE 24

MULTIPLY BY 12

X	0	1	2	3	4	5	6	7	8	9	10	11	12
12													

$$\begin{array}{r} 6 \\ \times\ 12 \\ \hline \end{array} \qquad \begin{array}{r} 1 \\ \times\ 12 \\ \hline \end{array} \qquad \begin{array}{r} 10 \\ \times\ 12 \\ \hline \end{array} \qquad \begin{array}{r} 11 \\ \times\ 12 \\ \hline \end{array} \qquad \begin{array}{r} 3 \\ \times\ 12 \\ \hline \end{array}$$

$$\begin{array}{r} 9 \\ \times\ 12 \\ \hline \end{array} \qquad \begin{array}{r} 12 \\ \times\ 0 \\ \hline \end{array} \qquad \begin{array}{r} 12 \\ \times\ 4 \\ \hline \end{array} \qquad \begin{array}{r} 12 \\ \times\ 9 \\ \hline \end{array} \qquad \begin{array}{r} 12 \\ \times\ 5 \\ \hline \end{array}$$

$$\begin{array}{r} 12 \\ \times\ 2 \\ \hline \end{array} \qquad \begin{array}{r} 8 \\ \times\ 12 \\ \hline \end{array} \qquad \begin{array}{r} 12 \\ \times\ 3 \\ \hline \end{array} \qquad \begin{array}{r} 12 \\ \times\ 6 \\ \hline \end{array} \qquad \begin{array}{r} 12 \\ \times\ 13 \\ \hline \end{array}$$

1 x 12 = _____   2 x 12 = _____   12 x 11 = _____

7 x 12 = _____   12 x 12 = _____   12 x 4 = _____

12 x 6 = _____   14 x 12 = _____   12 x 8 = _____

12 x 0 = _____   9 x 12 = _____   5 x 12 = _____

EXERCISE 25

MULTIPLICATION DRILLS! HOW MANY CAN YOU SOLVE IN A MINUTE?

1 x 2	3 x 2	11 x 3	2 x 9	10 x 13
4 x 6	9 x 8	2 x 3	12 x 6	2 x 5
6 x 7	1 x 4	7 x 3	12 x 4	8 x 1
5 x 9	2 x 3	10 x 9	5 x 8	2 x 5
3 x 4	0 x 9	6 x 5	3 x 6	7 x 11
10 x 12	9 x 5	55 x 0	6 x 6	2 x 2
5 x 3	7 x 11	8 x 3	1 x 6	8 x 7

EXERCISE 26

MULTIPLICATION DRILLS! HOW MANY CAN YOU SOLVE IN A MINUTE?

10 x 2	8 x 5	22 x 1	6 x 5	2 x 9
6 x 6	8 x 8	4 x 3	3 x 6	9 x 5
3 x 5	7 x 4	5 x 8	10 x 6	2 x 7
5 x 5	9 x 3	10 x 9	9 x 8	10 x 5
1 x 4	9 x 5	4 x 5	4 x 6	7 x 11
3 x 3	3 x 2	10 x 3	2 x 4	7 x 8
6 x 7	2 x 4	6 x 3	8 x 4	5 x 7

EXERCISE 27

MULTIPLICATION DRILLS! HOW MANY CAN YOU SOLVE IN A MINUTE?

7 × 7	9 × 5	3 × 4	5 × 6	9 × 9
5 × 10	8 × 9	2 × 3	2 × 6	8 × 5
1 × 7	7 × 5	4 × 8	9 × 6	2 × 7
0 × 6	9 × 2	11 × 9	6 × 8	0 × 5
8 × 6	2 × 2	6 × 5	3 × 6	7 × 11
5 × 5	8 × 7	11 × 3	2 × 9	10 × 11
4 × 2	6 × 1	7 × 3	12 × 4	7 × 7

EXERCISE 28

MULTIPLICATION DRILLS! HOW MANY CAN YOU SOLVE IN A MINUTE?

11	1	4	6	8
x 11	x 3	x 5	x 6	x 3

6	7	3	3	9
x 4	x 8	x 4	x 7	x 6

2	8	5	10	3
x 8	x 6	x 9	x 7	x 7

4	10	10	5	1
x 3	x 3	x 8	x 7	x 6

9	3	7	4	6
x 7	x 9	x 6	x 5	x 10

4	7	9	5	3
x 4	x 7	x 9	x 9	x 7

7	6	9	2	9
x 6	x 2	x 5	x 3	x 5

EXERCISE 29

FILL IN THE CORRECT ANSWER FOR EACH CIRCLE

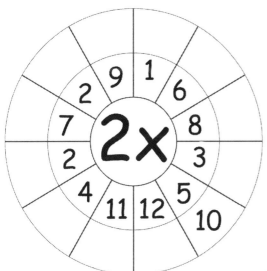

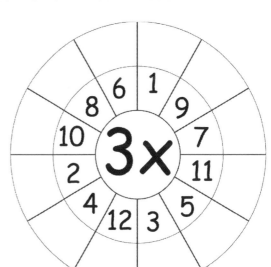

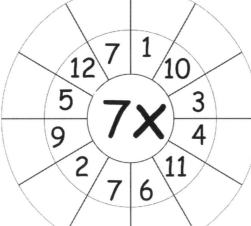

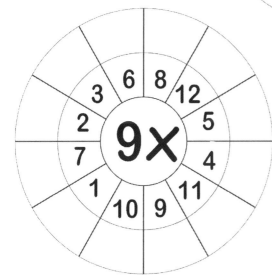

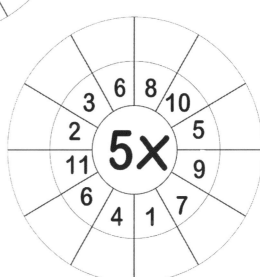

EXERCISE 30

FILL IN EACH SQUARE WITH FACTORS TO MAKE THE PRODUCTS IN GREY CORRECT

6	5	30
3	4	12
18	20	24

		24
		40
80	12	32

		18
		20
30	12	24

7		70
4		20
28	50	35

		48
		24
24	48	144

		48
		21
18	56	42

		18
		15
9	30	15

		10
		80
20	40	16

		18
		30
45	12	54

EXERCISE 31

FILL IN THE CORRECT ANSWER FOR EACH CIRCLE

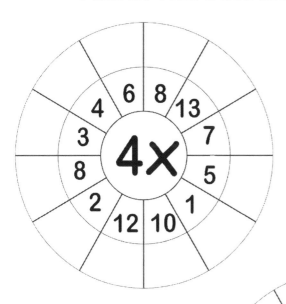

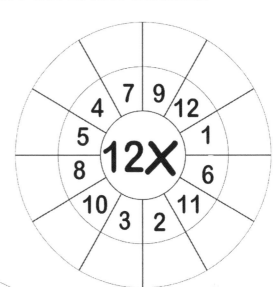

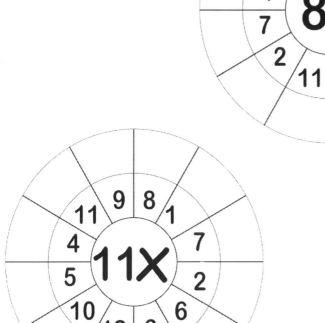

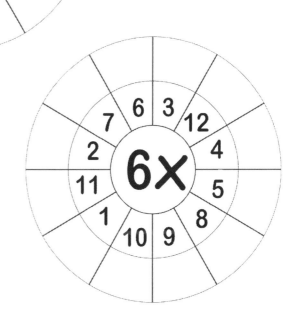

EXERCISE 32

FILL IN THE CORRECT ANSWER FOR EACH CIRCLE

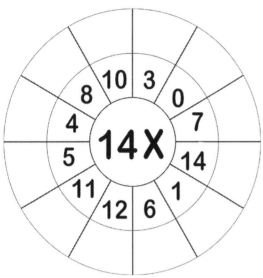

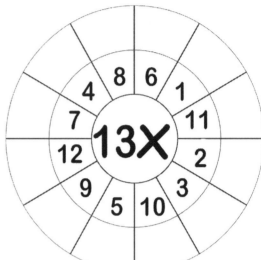

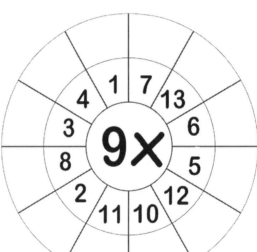

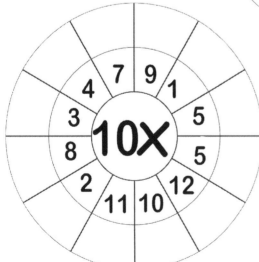

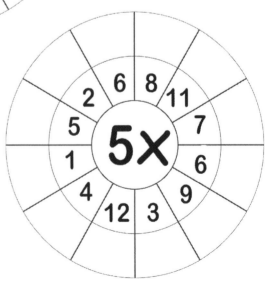

EXERCISE 33

SPEED ROUND! FILL IN THE FLOWERS WITH THE
CORRECT ANSWER AS FAST AS YOU CAN!

EXERCISE 34

MULTIPLICATION DRILLS! SOLVE THESE AS FAST AS YOU CAN!

31 x 51	31 x 93	74 x 55	16 x 16	48 x 53
56 x 64	77 x 78	773 x 4	3 x 557	29 x 76
12 x 38	68 x 96	55 x 59	150 x 27	35 x 71
24 x 32	120 x 43	140 x 18	175 x 37	41 x 46
31 x 21	61 x 93	44 x 75	15 x 15	33 x 88

EXERCISE 35

MULTIPLICATION DRILLS! SOLVE THESE AS FAST AS YOU CAN!

11	41	64	26	58
x 61	x 103	x 45	x 36	x 63

66	87	473	23	39
x 65	x 78	x 5	x 357	x 76

142	48	55	250	55
x 38	x 46	x 57	x 37	x 81

54	180	10	245	61
x 72	x 53	x 98	x 67	x 26

81	611	54	85	53
x 71	x 83	x 55	x 45	x 89

EXERCISE 36

MULTIPLICATION DRILLS! SOLVE THESE AS FAST AS YOU CAN!

61 x 32	71 x 73	84 x 25	46 x 76	88 x 69
76 x 15	37 x 68	973 x 25	13 x 357	309 x 76
132 x 28	8 x 46	57 x 5	250 x 17	25 x 31
44 x 62	130 x 33	80 x 28	45 x 67	601 x 26
801 x 71	211 x 3	55 x 55	86 x 65	93 x 89

EXERCISE 37

MULTIPLICATION DRILLS! SOLVE THESE AS FAST AS YOU CAN!

21	93	77	58	38
x 42	x 12	x 34	x 62	x 39

81	42	453	27	319
x 51	x 88	x 85	x 57	X 44

542	38	88	50	75
x 38	x 426	x 24	x 57	X 71

47	432	43	41	11
x 15	x 63	x 89	x 17	x 26

31	25	45	26	83
x 721	x 3·	x 54	x 25	x 81

EXERCISE 38

MULTIPLICATION DRILLS! SOLVE THESE AS FAST AS YOU CAN!

41 x 51	72 x 43	94 x 21	36 x 28	78 x 59
61 x 12	49 x 99	922 x 22	55 x 35	39 x 76
142 x 78	118 x 26	107 x 95	50 x 28	13 x 31
58 x 64	134 x 22	10 x 20	35 x 87	301 x 29
111 x 51	571 x 73	505 x 5	816 x 65	84 x 71

EXERCISE 39

MULTIPLICATION DRILLS! SOLVE THESE AS FAST AS YOU CAN!

51	82	24	67	80
x 81	x 93	x 51	x 13	x 33

72	59	12	15	59
x 25	x 9	x 72	x 45	x 96

121	128	187	60	144
x 50	x 36	x 35	x 18	x 2

123	14	103	353	391
x 7	x 12	x 20	x 87	x 49

151	371	475	306	64
x 51	x 21	x 37	x 35	x 21

EXERCISE 40

MULTIPLICATION DRILLS! SOLVE THESE AS FAST AS YOU CAN!

501	822	724	627	810
x 821	x 943	x 581	x 143	x 313

752	579	212	145	549
x 255	x 79	x 722	x 445	x 964

121	128	187	760	144
x 520	x 236	x 735	x 178	x 732

123	154	103	353	391
x 437	x 142	x 520	x 687	x 649

151	371	475	306	644
x 351	x 521	x 137	x 835	x 241

EXERCISE 41

MULTIPLICATION DRILLS! SOLVE THESE AS FAST AS YOU CAN!

221	722	724	678	181
x 721	x 973	x 511	x 143	x 613

752	579	212	145	649
x 255	x 79	x 722	x 445	x 924

131	228	177	260	111
x 120	x 826	x 635	x 398	x 111

321	122	134	341	181
x 123	x 444	x 790	x 587	x 340

771	272	145	236	546
x 771	x 447	x 227	x 733	x 353

EXERCISE 42

MULTIPLICATION DRILLS! SOLVE THESE AS FAST AS YOU CAN!

333 x 333	444 x 444	555 x 555	563 x 432	654 x 456
631 x 191	732 x 252	312 x 213	632 x 521	521 x 742
531 x 315	738 x 435	573 x 435	420 x 498	121 x 121
521 x 523	622 x 744	834 x 990	141 x 117	131 x 645
872 x 221	377 x 902	713 x 809	352 x 473	581 x 524

EXERCISE 43

MULTIPLICATION DRILLS! SOLVE THESE AS FAST AS YOU CAN!

237	884	545	316	2657
x 837	x 554	x 195	x 332	x 858

831	837	412	232	821
x 151	x 458	x 273	x 531	x 752

2551	778	1563	110	321
x 355	x 475	x 135	x 418	x 321

721	829	343	911	5435
x 723	x 791	x 280	x 817	x 446

3743	47	73	52	219
x 111	x 902	x 109	x 43	x 999

DIVISION BASICS

Division is the opposite, or inverse operation of multiplication. Division is an operation in which a quantity is divided (separated) into groups.

- Dividend – The quantity, or number, being divided.
- Divisor – The number that divides the dividend.
- Quotient – The number, not including any remainder, that results from dividing.
- Remainder – The amount left over when a number cannot be divided evenly.

Dividend
The number to be divided

Divisor
The number to be divided

Quotient
The answer

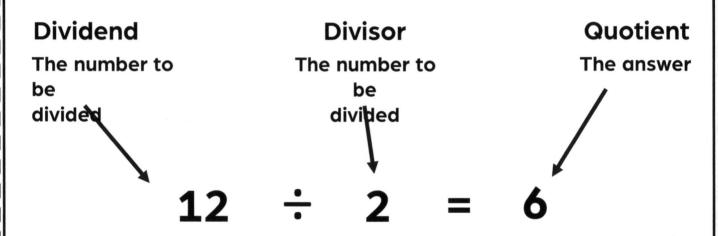

$$12 \div 2 = 6$$

Quotient

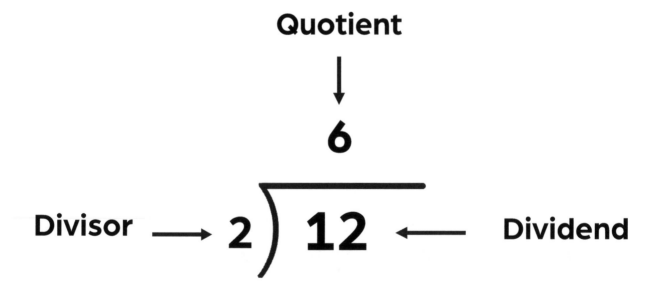

6

Divisor ⟶ 2 ⟌ 12 ⟵ Dividend

LEARNING DIVISION

Because division and multiplication are inverse operations, you can use your understanding of basic multiplication facts to learn basic division facts.

2 x 5 = 10	10 ÷ 2 = 5	10 ÷ 5 = 2
4 x 3 = 12	12 ÷ 4 = 3	12 ÷ 3 = 4
8 x 2 = 16	16 ÷ 8 = 2	16 ÷ 2 = 8
3 x 6 = 18	18 ÷ 3 = 6	18 ÷ 6 = 3
6 x 7 = 42	42 ÷ 6 = 7	42 ÷ 7 = 6

The division problem 16 ÷ 8 = 2 can also be written like the below example:

$$8 \overline{)16} \quad = 2$$

As you can see in this example, 16 is the dividend, 8 is the divisor and 2 is quotient.

> **Quick Tip!**
> You can check your answer to a division problem by multiplying the quotient by the divisor. The product should be equal to the dividend.

$$8 \overline{)16} = 2 \qquad 8 \ x \ 2 \ = \ 16$$

More examples below:

$$7 \overline{)49} = 7 \qquad 6 \overline{)24} = 4 \qquad 5 \overline{)50} = 10 \qquad 8 \overline{)72} = 9 \qquad 4 \overline{)36} = 9$$

GIVE IT A TRY!! PRACTICE TIME

1	2	3	4	5
$7 \overline{)28}$	$6 \overline{)12}$	$9 \overline{)54}$	$9 \overline{)99}$	$4 \overline{)32}$

MAKING SENSE OF LONG DIVISION

Long division is a method used when dividing a large number (usually three digits or more) by a two-digit (or more) number.

In the below example, we'll go through all the steps to find the answer.

$$15 \overline{) 3640}$$

$$\begin{array}{r} 2 \\ 15 \overline{) 3640} \\ -30 \\ \hline 6 \end{array}$$

1) 15 doesn't go into 3, so you have to look at the next digit.

2) 15 does go into 36, two times, so put a 2 above the 6.

$$15 \times 2 = 30$$

3) Subtract 30 from 36 to get the remainder.

$$36 - 30 = 6$$

$$\begin{array}{r} 24 \\ 15 \overline{) 3640} \\ -30 \downarrow \\ \hline 64 \\ -60 \\ \hline 4 \end{array}$$

4) Bring the 4 down to make 64. 15 goes into 64 four times. So, at the top, put a 4 above the 4.

$$15 \times 4 = 60$$

5) Subtract 60 from 64 to get the remainder.

$$64 - 60 = 4$$

$$\begin{array}{r} 242 \\ 15 \overline{) 3640} \\ -30 \\ \hline 64 \\ -60 \downarrow \\ \hline 40 \\ -30 \\ \hline 10 \end{array}$$

6) Bring the 0 down to make 40. 15 goes into 40 two times. So, at the top, put a 2 above the 0.

$$15 \times 2 = 30$$

7) Subtract 30 from 40 to get the remainder.

$$40 - 30 = 10$$

ANSWER

242 R 10

EXERCISE 44

UNDERSTANDING THE RELATIONSHIP BETWEEN DIVISION AND SUBTRACTION

How many times can 3 be subtracted from 12?

$$12 - 3 = 9$$
$$9 - 3 = 6$$
$$6 - 3 = 3$$
$$3 - 3 = 0$$

__3__ times

How many times can 4 be subtracted from 8?

_____ - _____ = _____
_____ - _____ = _____

_____ times

How many times can 6 be subtracted from 18?

_____ - _____ = _____
_____ - _____ = _____
_____ - _____ = _____

_____ times

How many times can 5 be subtracted from 25?

_____ - _____ = _____
_____ - _____ = _____
_____ - _____ = _____
_____ - _____ = _____
_____ - _____ = _____

_____ times

How many times can 2 be subtracted from 10?

_____ - _____ = _____
_____ - _____ = _____
_____ - _____ = _____
_____ - _____ = _____
_____ - _____ = _____

_____ times

EXERCISE 45

FILL IN THE BLANKS WITH 2 MULTIPLICATION AND 2 DIVISION FACTS

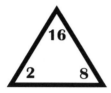

____ X ____ = ____

____ X ____ = ____

____ ÷ ____ = ____

____ ÷ ____ = ____

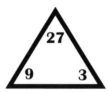

____ X ____ = ____

____ X ____ = ____

____ ÷ ____ = ____

____ ÷ ____ = ____

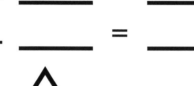

____ X ____ = ____

____ X ____ = ____

____ ÷ ____ = ____

____ ÷ ____ = ____

____ X ____ = ____

____ X ____ = ____

____ ÷ ____ = ____

____ ÷ ____ = ____

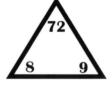

____ X ____ = ____

____ X ____ = ____

____ ÷ ____ = ____

____ ÷ ____ = ____

EXERCISE 46

SOLVE EACH ARRAY BELOW

1 △ △ △ △ △ △
△ △ △ △ △ △
△ △ △ △ △ △

$18 \div 2 =$ _____

2 △ △ △
△ △ △
△ △ △

$9 \div 3 =$ _____

3 △ △ △ △
△ △ △
△ △ △

$12 \div 3 =$ _____

4 △ △ △ △ △ △

$6 \div 1 =$ _____

5 △ △ △ △ △ △ △
△ △ △ △ △ △ △
△ △ △ △ △ △ △

$21 \div 3 =$ _____

6 △ △ △ △ △ △ △
△ △ △ △ △ △ △

$14 \div 2 =$ _____

7 △ △
△ △
△ △
△ △

$8 \div 2 =$ _____

8 △ △
△ △

$4 \div 2 =$ _____

EXERCISE 47

FILL IN THE BLANK WITH THE MISSING FACTOR

$2 \times \underline{\hspace{1cm}} = 2$ $2 \times \underline{\hspace{1cm}} = 32$ $2 \times \underline{\hspace{1cm}} = 8$

$2 \times \underline{\hspace{1cm}} = 28$ $2 \times \underline{\hspace{1cm}} = 24$ $2 \times \underline{\hspace{1cm}} = 20$

DIVIDE BY 2

$12 \div 2 = \underline{\hspace{1cm}}$ $22 \div 2 = \underline{\hspace{1cm}}$ $18 \div 2 = \underline{\hspace{1cm}}$

$16 \div 2 = \underline{\hspace{1cm}}$ $4 \div 2 = \underline{\hspace{1cm}}$ $20 \div 2 = \underline{\hspace{1cm}}$

$14 \div 2 = \underline{\hspace{1cm}}$ $24 \div 2 = \underline{\hspace{1cm}}$ $30 \div 2 = \underline{\hspace{1cm}}$

$6 \div 2 = \underline{\hspace{1cm}}$ $8 \div 2 = \underline{\hspace{1cm}}$ $2 \div 2 = \underline{\hspace{1cm}}$

1	2	3	4	5
$2\overline{)16}$	$2\overline{)18}$	$2\overline{)22}$	$2\overline{)26}$	$2\overline{)28}$

6	7	8	9	10
$2\overline{)10}$	$2\overline{)14}$	$2\overline{)20}$	$2\overline{)24}$	$2\overline{)8}$

11	12	13	14	15
$2\overline{)12}$	$2\overline{)16}$	$2\overline{)4}$	$2\overline{)30}$	$2\overline{)36}$

EXERCISE 48

FILL IN THE BLANK WITH THE MISSING FACTOR

$3 \times \underline{\hspace{1cm}} = 3$ $3 \times \underline{\hspace{1cm}} = 12$ $3 \times \underline{\hspace{1cm}} = 18$

$3 \times \underline{\hspace{1cm}} = 27$ $3 \times \underline{\hspace{1cm}} = 33$ $3 \times \underline{\hspace{1cm}} = 30$

DIVIDE BY 3

$36 \div 3 = \underline{\hspace{1cm}}$ $9 \div 3 = \underline{\hspace{1cm}}$ $24 \div 3 = \underline{\hspace{1cm}}$

$21 \div 3 = \underline{\hspace{1cm}}$ $18 \div 3 = \underline{\hspace{1cm}}$ $99 \div 3 = \underline{\hspace{1cm}}$

$15 \div 3 = \underline{\hspace{1cm}}$ $27 \div 3 = \underline{\hspace{1cm}}$ $30 \div 3 = \underline{\hspace{1cm}}$

$6 \div 3 = \underline{\hspace{1cm}}$ $15 \div 3 = \underline{\hspace{1cm}}$ $3 \div 3 = \underline{\hspace{1cm}}$

1	2	3	4	5
$3\overline{)18}$	$3\overline{)42}$	$3\overline{)39}$	$3\overline{)36}$	$3\overline{)27}$

6	7	8	9	10
$3\overline{)15}$	$3\overline{)3}$	$3\overline{)99}$	$3\overline{)24}$	$3\overline{)9}$

11	12	13	14	15
$3\overline{)21}$	$3\overline{)45}$	$3\overline{)48}$	$3\overline{)30}$	$3\overline{)33}$

EXERCISE 49

FILL IN THE BLANK WITH THE MISSING FACTOR

4 x _____ = 8   4 x _____ = 12   4 x _____ = 44

4 x _____ = 16   4 x _____ = 40   4 x _____ = 56

DIVIDE BY 4

36 ÷ 4 = _____	8 ÷ 4 = _____	24 ÷ 4 = _____
28 ÷ 4 = _____	32 ÷ 4 = _____	40 ÷ 4 = _____
36 ÷ 4 = _____	44 ÷ 4 = _____	52 ÷ 4 = _____
12 ÷ 4 = _____	16 ÷ 4 = _____	4 ÷ 4 = _____

1. 4)‾16‾

2. 4)‾20‾

3. 4)‾32‾

4. 4)‾36‾

5. 4)‾44‾

6. 4)‾48‾

7. 4)‾4‾

8. 4)‾24‾

9. 4)‾48‾

10. 4)‾8‾

11. 4)‾28‾

12. 4)‾12‾

13. 4)‾48‾

14. 4)‾32‾

15. 4)‾40‾

EXERCISE 50

FILL IN THE BLANK WITH THE MISSING FACTOR

$5 \times \underline{\hspace{1cm}} = 5$ $\qquad$ $5 \times \underline{\hspace{1cm}} = 10$ $\qquad$ $5 \times \underline{\hspace{1cm}} = 15$

$5 \times \underline{\hspace{1cm}} = 20$ $\qquad$ $5 \times \underline{\hspace{1cm}} = 30$ $\qquad$ $5 \times \underline{\hspace{1cm}} = 35$

DIVIDE BY 5

$40 \div 5 = \underline{\hspace{1cm}}$ $\qquad$ $5 \div 5 = \underline{\hspace{1cm}}$ $\qquad$ $95 \div 5 = \underline{\hspace{1cm}}$

$25 \div 5 = \underline{\hspace{1cm}}$ $\qquad$ $10 \div 5 = \underline{\hspace{1cm}}$ $\qquad$ $20 \div 5 = \underline{\hspace{1cm}}$

$15 \div 5 = \underline{\hspace{1cm}}$ $\qquad$ $45 \div 5 = \underline{\hspace{1cm}}$ $\qquad$ $30 \div 5 = \underline{\hspace{1cm}}$

$55 \div 5 = \underline{\hspace{1cm}}$ $\qquad$ $60 \div 5 = \underline{\hspace{1cm}}$ $\qquad$ $35 \div 5 = \underline{\hspace{1cm}}$

1	2	3	4	5
$5\overline{)40}$	$5\overline{)85}$	$5\overline{)70}$	$5\overline{)30}$	$5\overline{)25}$

6	7	8	9	10
$5\overline{)15}$	$5\overline{)5}$	$5\overline{)20}$	$5\overline{)45}$	$5\overline{)10}$

11	12	13	14	15
$5\overline{)55}$	$5\overline{)75}$	$5\overline{)80}$	$5\overline{)50}$	$5\overline{)60}$

EXERCISE 51

FILL IN THE BLANK WITH THE MISSING FACTOR

6 x _____ = 18   6 x _____ = 48   6 x _____ = 24

6 x _____ = 12   6 x _____ = 6   6 x _____ = 36

DIVIDE BY 6

$36 \div 6$ = _____ $6 \div 6$ = _____ $66 \div 6$ = _____

$12 \div 6$ = _____ $72 \div 6$ = _____ $78 \div 6$ = _____

$24 \div 6$ = _____ $30 \div 6$ = _____ $84 \div 6$ = _____

$54 \div 6$ = _____ $18 \div 6$ = _____ $90 \div 6$ = _____

1
$6 \overline{)18}$

2
$6 \overline{)42}$

3
$6 \overline{)36}$

4
$6 \overline{)42}$

5
$6 \overline{)78}$

6
$6 \overline{)30}$

7
$6 \overline{)6}$

8
$6 \overline{)84}$

9
$6 \overline{)24}$

10
$6 \overline{)90}$

11
$6 \overline{)48}$

12
$6 \overline{)54}$

13
$6 \overline{)12}$

14
$6 \overline{)96}$

15
$6 \overline{)66}$

EXERCISE 52

FILL IN THE BLANK WITH THE MISSING FACTOR

$7 \times$ _____ $= 14$ $7 \times$ _____ $= 21$ $7 \times$ _____ $= 28$

$7 \times$ _____ $= 42$ $7 \times$ _____ $= 84$ $7 \times$ _____ $= 49$

DIVIDE BY 7

$42 \div 7 =$ _____ $7 \div 7 \quad =$ _____ $28 \div 7 \quad =$ _____

$49 \div 7 =$ _____ $14 \div 7 \quad =$ _____ $35 \div 7 \quad =$ _____

$63 \div 7 =$ _____ $21 \div 7 \quad =$ _____ $56 \div 7 \quad =$ _____

$35 \div 7 =$ _____ $70 \div 7 \quad =$ _____ $77 \div 7 \quad =$ _____

1	2	3	4	5
$7 \overline{)91}$	$7 \overline{)105}$	$7 \overline{)70}$	$7 \overline{)63}$	$7 \overline{)84}$

6	7	8	9	10
$7 \overline{)21}$	$7 \overline{)28}$	$7 \overline{)49}$	$7 \overline{)77}$	$7 \overline{)35}$

11	12	13	14	15
$7 \overline{)70}$	$7 \overline{)91}$	$7 \overline{)14}$	$7 \overline{)42}$	$7 \overline{)14}$

EXERCISE 53

FILL IN THE BLANK WITH THE MISSING FACTOR

8 x _____ = 80   8 x _____ = 96   8 x _____ = 32

8 x _____ = 40   8 x _____ = 56   8 x _____ = 16

DIVIDE BY 8

$72 \div 8$ = _____ | $8 \div 8$ = _____ | $56 \div 8$ = _____

$24 \div 8$ = _____ | $32 \div 8$ = _____ | $40 \div 8$ = _____

$16 \div 8$ = _____ | $48 \div 8$ = _____ | $64 \div 8$ = _____

$80 \div 8$ = _____ | $88 \div 8$ = _____ | $96 \div 8$ = _____

1. $8 \overline{)48}$

2. $8 \overline{)40}$

3. $8 \overline{)96}$

4. $8 \overline{)88}$

5. $8 \overline{)56}$

6. $8 \overline{)16}$

7. $8 \overline{)64}$

8. $8 \overline{)24}$

9. $8 \overline{)32}$

10. $8 \overline{)72}$

11. $8 \overline{)80}$

12. $8 \overline{)8}$

13. $8 \overline{)48}$

14. $8 \overline{)104}$

15. $8 \overline{)112}$

EXERCISE 54

FILL IN THE BLANK WITH THE MISSING FACTOR

$9 \times \underline{\hspace{1cm}} = 9$ $9 \times \underline{\hspace{1cm}} = 36$ $9 \times \underline{\hspace{1cm}} = 54$

$9 \times \underline{\hspace{1cm}} = 45$ $9 \times \underline{\hspace{1cm}} = 81$ $9 \times \underline{\hspace{1cm}} = 36$

DIVIDE BY 9

$36 \div 9 = \underline{\hspace{1cm}}$ $9 \div 9 = \underline{\hspace{1cm}}$ $18 \div 9 = \underline{\hspace{1cm}}$

$108 \div 9 = \underline{\hspace{1cm}}$ $99 \div 9 = \underline{\hspace{1cm}}$ $54 \div 9 = \underline{\hspace{1cm}}$

$63 \div 9 = \underline{\hspace{1cm}}$ $27 \div 9 = \underline{\hspace{1cm}}$ $81 \div 9 = \underline{\hspace{1cm}}$

$72 \div 9 = \underline{\hspace{1cm}}$ $90 \div 9 = \underline{\hspace{1cm}}$ $36 \div 9 = \underline{\hspace{1cm}}$

1	2	3	4	5
$9\overline{)54}$	$9\overline{)90}$	$9\overline{)18}$	$9\overline{)36}$	$9\overline{)99}$

6	7	8	9	10
$9\overline{)27}$	$9\overline{)45}$	$9\overline{)108}$	$9\overline{)72}$	$9\overline{)27}$

11	12	13	14	15
$9\overline{)81}$	$9\overline{)63}$	$9\overline{)54}$	$9\overline{)18}$	$9\overline{)36}$

EXERCISE 55

FILL IN THE BLANK WITH THE MISSING FACTOR

10 x _____ = 10   10 x _____ = 20   10 x _____ = 180

10 x _____ = 270   10 x _____ = 330   10 x _____ = 30

DIVIDE BY 10

10 ÷ 10 = _____   50 ÷ 10 = _____   60 ÷ 10 = _____

20 ÷ 10 = _____   70 ÷ 10 = _____   110 ÷ 10 = _____

40 ÷ 10 = _____   90 ÷ 10 = _____   80 ÷ 10 = _____

30 ÷ 10 = _____   100 ÷ 10 = _____   120 ÷ 10 = _____

---

1. $10\overline{)180}$ 2. $10\overline{)40}$ 3. $10\overline{)30}$ 4. $10\overline{)50}$ 5. $10\overline{)70}$

6. $10\overline{)60}$ 7. $10\overline{)10}$ 8. $10\overline{)80}$ 9. $10\overline{)20}$ 10. $10\overline{)110}$

11. $10\overline{)120}$ 12. $10\overline{)90}$ 13. $10\overline{)100}$ 14. $10\overline{)30}$ 15. $10\overline{)300}$

EXERCISE 56

FILL IN THE BLANK WITH THE MISSING FACTOR

11 x _____ = 11   11 x _____ = 33   11 x _____ = 99

11 x _____ = 22   11 x _____ = 66   11 x _____ = 55

DIVIDE BY 11

$55 \div 11 =$ _____ | $66 \div 11 =$ _____ | $121 \div 11 =$ _____

$22 \div 11 =$ _____ | $77 \div 11 =$ _____ | $132 \div 11 =$ _____

$88 \div 11 =$ _____ | $44 \div 11 =$ _____ | $88 \div 11 =$ _____

$33 \div 11 =$ _____ | $99 \div 11 =$ _____ | $11 \div 11 =$ _____

1	2	3	4	5
11) 154	11) 176	11) 22	11) 44	11) 33

6	7	8	9	10
11) 77	11) 99	11) 88	11) 66	11) 110

11	12	13	14	15
11) 88	11) 22	11) 55	11) 99	11) 11

EXERCISE 57

FILL IN THE BLANK WITH THE MISSING FACTOR

12 x ____ = 12   12 x ____ = 36   12 x ____ = 96

12 x ____ = 24   12 x ____ = 48   12 x ____ = 84

DIVIDE BY 12

24 ÷ 12 = ____   72 ÷ 12 = ____   60 ÷ 12 = ____

0 ÷ 12 = ____   12 ÷ 12 = ____   120 ÷ 12 = ____

60 ÷ 12 = ____   96 ÷ 12 = ____   36 ÷ 12 = ____

84 ÷ 12 = ____   132 ÷ 12 = ____   48 ÷ 12 = ____

1. 12)‾168‾

2. 12)‾120‾

3. 12)‾156‾

4. 12)‾72‾

5. 12)‾12‾

6. 12)‾84‾

7. 12)‾108‾

8. 12)‾36‾

9. 12)‾144‾

10. 12)‾180‾

11. 12)‾96‾

12. 12)‾60‾

13. 12)‾132‾

14. 12)‾24‾

15. 12)‾84‾

EXERCISE 58

FILL IN THE BLANK WITH THE MISSING FACTOR

13 x _____ = 78 | 13 x _____ = 91 | 13 x _____ = 52

13 x _____ = 130 | 13 x _____ = 39 | 13 x _____ = 26

DIVIDE BY 13

65 ÷ 13 = _____ | 143 ÷ 13 = _____ | 52 ÷ 13 = _____

182 ÷ 13 = _____ | 104 ÷ 13 = _____ | 26 ÷ 13 = _____

91 ÷ 13 = _____ | 0 ÷ 13 = _____ | 39 ÷ 13 = _____

156 ÷ 13 = _____ | 26 ÷ 13 = _____ | 13 ÷ 13 = _____

1	2	3	4	5
13)117	13)195	13)39	13)130	13)13

6	7	8	9	10
13)104	13)156	13)52	13)26	13)169

11	12	13	14	15
13)182	13)91	13)0	13)65	13)117

EXERCISE 59

FILL IN THE BLANK WITH THE MISSING FACTOR

14 x _____ = 168   14 x _____ = 14   14 x _____ = 182

14 x _____ = 126   14 x _____ = 28   14 x _____ = 196

DIVIDE BY 14

84 ÷ 14 = _____   140 ÷ 14 = _____   210 ÷ 14 = _____

42 ÷ 14 = _____   70 ÷ 14 = _____   168 ÷ 14 = _____

56 ÷ 14 = _____   98 ÷ 14 = _____   140 ÷ 14 = _____

154 ÷ 14 = _____   28 ÷ 14 = _____   182 ÷ 14 = _____

1. 14) 112   2. 14) 196   3. 14) 70   4. 14) 168   5. 14) 42

6. 14) 14   7. 14) 0   8. 14) 210   9. 14) 182   10. 14) 126

11. 14) 84   12. 14) 98   13. 14) 56   14. 14) 140   15. 14) 154

EXERCISE 60

FUN WITH DIVISION WORD PROBLEMS

1) 9 Brownies shared by 3 best friends. Draw the brownies below.

How many brownies does each friend get?

_____

Write the division for the word problem

_____

2) 6 marbles shared by 2 siblings. Draw the marbles below.

How many marbles does each sibling get?

_____

Write the division for the word problem

_____

3) 24 pieces of candy shared amongst 6 classmates.

How many pieces of candy does each classmate get?

_____

Write the division for the word problem

_____

4) 8 milk bones shared between 2 dogs.

How many milk bones does each classmate dog?

_____

Write the division for the word problem

_____

EXERCISE 61

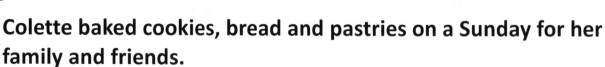

÷ DIVISION WORD PROBLEMS ÷

Colette baked cookies, bread and pastries on a Sunday for her family and friends.

1). She made 47 gingerbread cookies which she'll distribute equally into glass jars. If each jar will contain six cookies each, how many cookies will not be placed in a jar?

2). She also prepared 59 doughnuts which she plans to give to her 8 neighbors. If each neighbor receives an equal number of doughnuts, how many will Colette have left?

3). Colette also baked chocolate chip cookies for her 30 classmates. If she can place 12 cookies on a tray at a time, how many trays will she need to prepare 276 cookies at a time?

4). Colette's friends are coming over in the afternoon, so she made 420 tiny pretzels. If one serving is equal to 12 pretzels, how many servings of tiny pretzels did Colette prepare?

5). She baked 53 blueberry cupcakes for the preschool children down the street. If two lemon cupcakes were left at home, how many boxes with 3 lemon cupcakes each were given away?

EXERCISE 62

÷ DIVISION WORD PROBLEMS ÷

Julie and her family had a long list of activities this past weekend.

1). Julie prepared 74 crepes for breakfast. If the crepes were served equally to 12 people, how many crepes were left uneaten?

2). Julie and her sister rounded up all 98 of their dolls and placed them on the shelves in the basement. If every shelf is 4 feet wide and can only hold a maximum of 7 dolls, how many shelves will be filled?

3). The family collected all of the family pictures to place them in an album. If an album can contain 20 pictures, how many albums will they need if there are 480 pictures?

4). Julie's little brother Mike, collected 89 baseball cards in his room and put them in boxes. If a box can hold a maximum of 8 cards, how many full boxes are there? How many cards are left over?

5). Julie's grandfather repaired the bookshelves in the living room. If he has 210 books to be placed equally on 10 shelves, how many books will each shelf have? Are there any books leftover?

EXERCISE 63

÷ DIVISION WORD PROBLEMS ÷

Sophie is going to give away some of her toys to an orphanage.

1). Nine of the children like stickers. If she plans to give all of them an equal number of stickers, if she has 72 stickers, how many will each receive?

2). There are 5 boys who love to play with marbles. If Sophie has 35 marbles, how many marbles will each boy receive?

3). Sometimes Sophie does origami with the kids. If she has 48 origami papers to share, how many will each receive if everyone gets the same number of origami papers?

4). One of the children has a large bag of bouncy balls under her bed. She decided to share them with the other children by placing them in bags. If every bag can hold 4 balls and Sophie has 36 bouncy balls, how many bags will be used?

5). At home Sophie has 63 used notebooks in her desk. She plans to recycle them all. If she places them in boxes which can hold 9 notebooks each, write an equation for the number of boxes she will use.

EXERCISE 64

÷ ADVANCED DIVISION WORD PROBLEMS ÷

A group of friends have an upcoming book report.

1). Joseph loves reading about the deep ocean. He read 10 pages a day of a book which has 120 pages. How many days did it take Joseph to finish reading the book?

2). Gary wanted to learn about hydroelectric power, so he read 8 pages a day of a 99 page book on the subject. How many days did it take Gary to finish the book? How many pages did he read on the last day?

3). Alexa read a 43 page book about classical music. If she read only 3 pages a day, how many days will it take Alexa to finish reading the book? How many pages did she read on the last day?

4). Stefan read a 240 page book. Each day, he spent 3 hours reading it. If he read the same number of pages for 12 days, how many pages did he read every day?

5). Ira was fascinated with the history of the Silk Road. He read 11 pages per hour of the book "Discovering the Silk Road". If the book has 143 pages, how many hours did it take Ira to finish reading the book?

EXERCISE 65

÷ ADVANCED DIVISION & MULTIPLICATION WORD PROBLEMS ÷

A beautiful hotel right next to the beach has 7 floors. The gym, restaurant and lobby are all on the ground floor. The guestrooms are on 1st through 6th floors.

1). If there are 35 basic rooms on each floor, how many basic rooms are there?

2). On each floor there are 4 housekeepers. One of the rooms only requires one housekeeper. If the housekeepers distribute the work equally, how many housekeepers need to clean more rooms than the others?

3). If each basic room can fit 2 guests, what is the maximum number of guests that all the basic rooms can accommodate?

4). The hotel has 18 suites in total, how many suites are there on each floor if each floor has the same floorplan?

5). Each suite has 3 beds, of which each bed also has a nightstand on each side. How many bed nightstands are there in all the suites combined?

6). Write an equation for the problem below using "x". Solve the equation after.
A basic room in the hotel is $250 dollars per night. A couple stayed in a basic room for X nights. Their total charge for the room was $750.

EXERCISE 66

÷ **ADVANCED DIVISION & MULTIPLICATION WORD PROBLEMS** ÷

Oakdale Hospital has 9 doctors, 101 nurses and 26 wards.

1). How many beds are there in total if each ward has 16 beds?

2). Each doctor has assistance from at least one nurse. If the nurses are equally assigned to the doctors, about how many nurses are assigned to most doctors?

3). Some doctors receive help from more than one nurse. How many doctors are being assisted by one extra nurse?

4). How many nurses are working in the ward in total, if each ward requires 3 nurses to be on duty?

5). The hospital has 3 operating rooms. Each operating room requires 2 doctors and 4 nurses. How many medical staff are needed for all three operating rooms?

6). Write an equation for the problem below using "x". Solve the equation after.
There are X number of patients at Oakdale. Therefore, each doctor is responsible for 47 patients.

EXERCISE 67

÷ ADVANCED DIVISION & MULTIPLICATION WORD PROBLEMS ÷

Freddy's Fire Station has 9 fire trucks and 5 ambulances.

1). Each time an ambulance is dispatched, 3 paramedics are needed. How many paramedics are required to be on duty at any given time?

2). Suppose there are 3 different shifts for paramedics, how many total paramedics are there?

3). Each 12-hour shift has 54 active firefighters on duty. How many firefighters can be assigned equally to each firetruck?

4). How many firefighters will be working at Freddy's Fire Station everyday?

5). Every time there is a car accident, the fire station will send out 12 firefighters, 2 firetrucks and 1 ambulance. In the unfortunate event that there are 4 car accidents at the same time, how many firefighters will be dispatched?

6). Write an equation for the problem below using "x". Solve the equation after.
Being a firefighter can be tough work. Every 3 months, each firefighter needs to get 15 hours of additional training. Each firefighter is required to finish X hours of training every year.

÷ ADVANCED DIVISION & MULTIPLICATION WORD PROBLEMS ÷

Reliable Car Factory is open 12 hours a day and has 8 assembly lines. Each assembly line manufactures cars at the same speed.

1). Suppose there are 2 supervisors and 12 factory workers on each assembly line, how many workers are there in total?

2). If Reliable Car Factory produces 48 cars in a day, how many cars does each assembly line make each day?

3). If each assembly line operates for 12 hours a day, how long does it take for one assembly line to produce one car?

4). Reliable Car Factory pays each supervisor $30 per hour and the factory workers $80 per day. How much does a supervisor get paid each day?

5). What is the dollar amount in a day Reliable Car Factory has to pay for the total salary for all the workers?

6). Write an equation for the problem below using "x". Solve the equation after.
Reliable Car Factory received an order to manufacture X cars and the order is completed in 18 days.

EXERCISE 69

÷ ADVANCED DIVISION & FRACTION WORD PROBLEMS ÷

Construction Time!

1). A team of 7 construction workers collaborated to build 3 sheds in 10 days. How much of a shed did each of them build?

2). An 80-meter bridge was built in a total of 12 weeks. On average, how much of the bridge was built each week?

3). A 4-story building is 29 feet tall. Between which two whole numbers does the height of each story lie?

4). To pave 50 meters of road, it takes 14 tons of cement. How much of a road can be paved by using one ton of cement?

5). In order to build 4 flowerbeds, it takes 45 planks. Between which two numbers does the number of planks used for each flowerbed lie?

6). An old factory building was demolished recently. 5 dump trucks were used to transport a total of 2 tons of rubble. How much rubble did each truck carry?

EXERCISE 70

÷ ADVANCED DIVISION & FRACTION WORD PROBLEMS ÷

Recipes!

1). Colton used 3 packages of macaroni noodles to make dinner for 19 guests. How much did each guest have?

2). A delicious cupcake recipe calls for 190 grams of sugar to make 9 cupcakes. Between which two whole numbers does the weight of sugar used for each cupcake lie?

3). A 2-liter pitcher of apple juice is poured into 8 kid cups. How much apple juice is in each cup?

4). Colton's mother bought doughnuts for the family to share. There are 9 donuts total in the box. Colton's family consists of his mom, dad and two sisters. Including Colton, they are all sharing the doughnuts equally. How many donuts does each person get?

5). Their Grandma baked 38 cookies and her three grandkids shared the cookies equally. Between which two whole numbers does the number of cookies they have lie?

6). Mrs. Morgan made 4 pizzas with 11 oz. of cheese. How much cheese is each pizza made with?

EXERCISE 71

÷ ADVANCED DIVISION & FRACTION WORD PROBLEMS ÷

A little bit of this, a little bit of that...

1). Eva's math test has 22 questions on it. She's allowed 50 minutes to take the test. Between which two numbers does the time allowed for each question lie?

2). Mr. Bounds has 6 stacks of construction paper for his class of 17 students. How many stacks of construction paper does each student get?

3). Cool School Cafeteria prepared 13 large bowls of mixed fruit for 4 classes of 5th Grade students. How many mixed fruit bowls will each class get?

4). Beverly's class is going on a field trip to the museum. The transportation costs for the trip is $243. This cost will be shared between 5 classes. Between which two numbers does the fee each class needs to pay lie?

5). The school administrator ordered 6 boxes of supplies for the new school year. Cool School has 33 teachers. If the supplies are divided equally among the teachers, how many boxes of supplies will each teacher get?

6). The class library has 125 books for a class of 30 students. Between which two numbers does the number of books each student can borrow lie?

EXERCISE 72

FUN WITH DIVISION! SOLVE AS FAST AS YOU CAN!

$150 \div 10 =$ _____

$24 \div 8 =$ _____

$130 \div 10 =$ _____

$0 \div 4 =$ _____

$0 \div 8 =$ _____

$1 \div 1 =$ _____

$32 \div 4 =$ _____

$32 \div 8 =$ _____

$81 \div 9 =$ _____

$48 \div 4 =$ _____

$30 \div 2 =$ _____

$60 \div 10 =$ _____

$0 \div 2 =$ _____

$44 \div 4 =$ _____

$77 \div 7 =$ _____

$90 \div 9 =$ _____

$35 \div 7 =$ _____

$15 \div 5 =$ _____

$120 \div 8 =$ _____

$6 \div 1 =$ _____

$110 \div 10 =$ _____

$30 \div 5 =$ _____

$66 \div 6 =$ _____

$0 \div 9 =$ _____

$60 \div 5 =$ _____

$78 \div 6 =$ _____

$98 \div 7 =$ _____

$20 \div 10 =$ _____

$48 \div 8 =$ _____

$18 \div 2 =$ _____

$60 \div 4 =$ _____

$65 \div 5 =$ _____

$75 \div 5 =$ _____

$22 \div 2 =$ _____

$84 \div 6 =$ _____

$9 \div 9 =$ _____

$6 \div 2 =$ _____

$0 \div 10 =$ _____

$126 \div 9 =$ _____

$14 \div 2 =$ _____

$36 \div 9 =$ _____

$11 \div 1 =$ _____

$8 \div 1 =$ _____

$8 \div 8 =$ _____

$0 \div 5 =$ _____

EXERCISE 73

FUN WITH DIVISION! SOLVE AS FAST AS YOU CAN!

$4\overline{)24}$	$7\overline{)77}$	$5\overline{)50}$	$2\overline{)24}$	$3\overline{)15}$	$6\overline{)72}$	$6\overline{)48}$
$8\overline{)88}$	$4\overline{)36}$	$2\overline{)4}$	$6\overline{)66}$	$5\overline{)55}$	$3\overline{)36}$	$9\overline{)36}$
$2\overline{)16}$	$5\overline{)30}$	$2\overline{)10}$	$10\overline{)100}$	$10\overline{)110}$	$4\overline{)16}$	$10\overline{)20}$
$7\overline{)21}$	$7\overline{)63}$	$3\overline{)18}$	$3\overline{)30}$	$4\overline{)32}$	$8\overline{)24}$	$6\overline{)18}$
$8\overline{)48}$	$8\overline{)96}$	$9\overline{)18}$	$9\overline{)63}$	$6\overline{)60}$	$7\overline{)14}$	$2\overline{)6}$
$4\overline{)24}$	$7\overline{)77}$	$5\overline{)50}$	$2\overline{)24}$	$3\overline{)15}$	$6\overline{)72}$	$6\overline{)48}$
$8\overline{)88}$	$4\overline{)36}$	$2\overline{)4}$	$6\overline{)66}$	$5\overline{)55}$	$3\overline{)36}$	$9\overline{)36}$
$2\overline{)16}$	$5\overline{)30}$	$2\overline{)10}$	$10\overline{)100}$	$10\overline{)110}$	$4\overline{)16}$	$10\overline{)20}$

EXERCISE 74

FUN WITH DIVISION! SOLVE AS FAST AS YOU CAN!

$3 \div 1 =$ _____

$6 \div 1 =$ _____

$20 \div 4 =$ _____

$60 \div 10 =$ _____

$10 \div 5 =$ _____

$40 \div 8 =$ _____

$150 \div 10 =$ _____

$4 \div 4 =$ _____

$36 \div 3 =$ _____

$140 \div 10 =$ _____

$27 \div 3 =$ _____

$30 \div 10 =$ _____

$13 \div 1 =$ _____

$56 \div 4 =$ _____

$10 \div 1 =$ _____

$35 \div 7 =$ _____

$28 \div 7 =$ _____

$90 \div 6 =$ _____

$1 \div 1 =$ _____

$12 \div 6 =$ _____

$18 \div 3 =$ _____

$0 \div 8 =$ _____

$5 \div 5 =$ _____

$36 \div 9 =$ _____

$42 \div 7 =$ _____

$15 \div 5 =$ _____

$28 \div 4 =$ _____

$0 \div 9 =$ _____

$20 \div 10 =$ _____

$30 \div 3 =$ _____

$36 \div 6 =$ _____

$0 \div 10 =$ _____

$45 \div 5 =$ _____

$36 \div 4 =$ _____

$12 \div 2 =$ _____

$0 \div 1 =$ _____

$0 \div 2 =$ _____

$10 \div 10 =$ _____

$126 \div 9 =$ _____

$60 \div 6 =$ _____

$99 \div 9 =$ _____

$72 \div 9 =$ _____

$81 \div 9 =$ _____

$50 \div 10 =$ _____

$12 \div 4 =$ _____

EXERCISE 75

FUN WITH DIVISION! SOLVE AS FAST AS YOU CAN!

$4\overline{)24}$	$7\overline{)77}$	$5\overline{)50}$	$2\overline{)24}$	$3\overline{)15}$	$6\overline{)72}$	$6\overline{)48}$
$8\overline{)88}$	$4\overline{)36}$	$2\overline{)4}$	$6\overline{)66}$	$5\overline{)55}$	$3\overline{)36}$	$9\overline{)36}$
$2\overline{)16}$	$5\overline{)30}$	$2\overline{)10}$	$10\overline{)100}$	$10\overline{)110}$	$4\overline{)16}$	$10\overline{)20}$
$7\overline{)21}$	$7\overline{)63}$	$3\overline{)18}$	$3\overline{)30}$	$4\overline{)32}$	$8\overline{)24}$	$6\overline{)18}$
$8\overline{)48}$	$8\overline{)96}$	$9\overline{)18}$	$9\overline{)63}$	$6\overline{)60}$	$7\overline{)14}$	$2\overline{)6}$
$4\overline{)36}$	$5\overline{)10}$	$9\overline{)36}$	$11\overline{)55}$	$4\overline{)20}$	$2\overline{)14}$	$6\overline{)30}$
$8\overline{)24}$	$10\overline{)30}$	$3\overline{)27}$	$8\overline{)16}$	$11\overline{)88}$	$5\overline{)50}$	$3\overline{)9}$
$8\overline{)40}$	$7\overline{)77}$	$4\overline{)16}$	$10\overline{)60}$	$2\overline{)18}$	$2\overline{)6}$	$5\overline{)55}$

EXERCISE 76

FUN WITH DIVISION! SOLVE AS FAST AS YOU CAN!

$78 \div 6 =$ _____	$13 \div 1 =$ _____	$21 \div 7 =$ _____
$7 \div 1 =$ _____	$15 \div 3 =$ _____	$9 \div 3 =$ _____
$18 \div 9 =$ _____	$48 \div 8 =$ _____	$90 \div 9 =$ _____
$36 \div 9 =$ _____	$8 \div 8 =$ _____	$18 \div 6 =$ _____
$48 \div 4 =$ _____	$60 \div 5 =$ _____	$10 \div 10 =$ _____
$45 \div 3 =$ _____	$140 \div 10 =$ _____	$54 \div 6 =$ _____
$27 \div 9 =$ _____	$24 \div 8 =$ _____	$28 \div 4 =$ _____
$18 \div 3 =$ _____	$4 \div 4 =$ _____	$8 \div 4 =$ _____
$0 \div 7 =$ _____	$70 \div 5 =$ _____	$0 \div 3 =$ _____
$9 \div 1 =$ _____	$104 \div 8 =$ _____	$72 \div 9 =$ _____
$56 \div 8 =$ _____	$56 \div 7 =$ _____	$24 \div 6 =$ _____
$64 \div 8 =$ _____	$55 \div 5 =$ _____	$8 \div 1 =$ _____
$66 \div 6 =$ _____	$50 \div 5 =$ _____	$10 \div 1 =$ _____
$16 \div 4 =$ _____	$96 \div 8 =$ _____	$30 \div 2 =$ _____
$49 \div 7 =$ _____	$28 \div 2 =$ _____	$33 \div 3 =$ _____

EXERCISE 77

FUN WITH LONG DIVISION!

$2\overline{)152}$ $2\overline{)222}$ $17\overline{)833}$ $75\overline{)900}$

$4\overline{)724}$ $6\overline{)258}$ $5\overline{)280}$ $74\overline{)444}$

$5\overline{)620}$ $6\overline{)630}$ $75\overline{)375}$ $4\overline{)64}$

$4\overline{)220}$ $8\overline{)680}$ $22\overline{)66}$ $98\overline{)980}$

EXERCISE 78

FUN WITH LONG DIVISION!

$8\overline{)656}$ $\qquad$ $2\overline{)862}$ $\qquad$ $8\overline{)576}$ $\qquad$ $9\overline{)234}$

$9\overline{)351}$ $\qquad$ $3\overline{)207}$ $\qquad$ $3\overline{)534}$ $\qquad$ $5\overline{)685}$

$4\overline{)144}$ $\qquad$ $8\overline{)856}$ $\qquad$ $3\overline{)615}$ $\qquad$ $5\overline{)110}$

$8\overline{)816}$ $\qquad$ $6\overline{)714}$ $\qquad$ $6\overline{)822}$ $\qquad$ $8\overline{)200}$

EXERCISE 79

FUN WITH LONG DIVISION!

$19{\overline{)45}}$ $49{\overline{)83}}$ $9{\overline{)47}}$ $7{\overline{)69}}$

$82{\overline{)216}}$ $9{\overline{)868}}$ $50{\overline{)234}}$ $6{\overline{)462}}$

$9{\overline{)90}}$ $5{\overline{)11}}$ $66{\overline{)87}}$ $2{\overline{)56}}$

$62{\overline{)80}}$ $84{\overline{)99}}$ $7{\overline{)77}}$ $96{\overline{)99}}$

EXERCISE 80

FUN WITH LONG DIVISION!

$68\overline{)453}$ $54\overline{)307}$ $63\overline{)836}$ $70\overline{)830}$

$33\overline{)955}$ $76\overline{)106}$ $54\overline{)271}$ $90\overline{)889}$

$46\overline{)250}$ $33\overline{)905}$ $72\overline{)795}$ $51\overline{)691}$

EXERCISE 81

FUN WITH LONG DIVISION!

$40\overline{)939}$ $20\overline{)156}$ $69\overline{)732}$ $21\overline{)883}$

$82\overline{)880}$ $49\overline{)785}$ $46\overline{)302}$ $68\overline{)308}$

$64\overline{)128}$ $92\overline{)766}$ $63\overline{)525}$ $16\overline{)586}$

EXERCISE 82

FUN WITH LONG DIVISION!

$$66\overline{)2{,}683}$$

$$56\overline{)552}$$

$$67\overline{)249}$$

$$20\overline{)366}$$

$$13\overline{)5{,}168}$$

$$14\overline{)3{,}770}$$

$$14\overline{)1{,}363}$$

$$31\overline{)1{,}875}$$

$$74\overline{)7{,}444}$$

EXERCISE 83

FUN WITH LONG DIVISION!

$82\overline{)5{,}008}$ $95\overline{)3{,}817}$ $75\overline{)829}$

$9\overline{)4{,}253}$ $60\overline{)314}$ $5\overline{)511}$

$44\overline{)6{,}446}$ $4\overline{)253}$ $35\overline{)785}$

EXERCISE 84

FUN WITH LONG DIVISION!

$637 \overline{)9,171}$

$915 \overline{)925}$

$19 \overline{)430}$

$810 \overline{)7,669}$

$87 \overline{)896}$

$451 \overline{)6,286}$

EXERCISE 85

FUN WITH LONG DIVISION!

$791\overline{)8,135}$ $845\overline{)8,251}$

$11\overline{)3,064}$ $829\overline{)829}$

$74\overline{)5,842}$ $85\overline{)849}$

EXERCISE 86

LET'S COLOR WITH BASIC DIVISION!

Coloring Key:

Blue 2   Tan 3   Black 4   Black 5

6÷3	12÷6	6÷3	6÷3	6÷3	18÷9	8÷4	2÷1	20÷10	10÷5	4÷2	10÷5	18÷9	20÷10	2÷1	12÷6	16÷8	2÷1	6÷3
4÷2	12÷6	6÷3	20÷10	10÷5	12÷6	18÷9	18÷9	14÷7	4÷2	14÷7	12÷6	18÷9	18÷9	2÷1	6÷3	2÷1	14÷7	8÷4
20÷10	10÷5	20÷10	20÷10	6÷3	8÷4	12÷6	2÷1	18÷9	10÷5	18÷6	14÷7	6÷3	14÷7	12÷4	16÷8	8÷4	18÷9	4÷2
10÷5	8÷4	6÷3	14÷7	8÷4	18÷9	18÷9	16÷8	10÷5	4÷2	20÷4	50÷10	30÷6	10÷2	40÷8	4÷2	12÷6	18÷9	20÷10
4÷2	4÷2	12÷6	4÷2	6÷3	4÷2	10÷5	10÷5	8÷4	6÷3	15÷3	12÷3	25÷5	8÷2	10÷2	16÷8	18÷9	6÷3	16÷8
10÷5	20÷10	20÷10	6÷3	20÷10	12÷6	14÷7	14÷7	20÷10	20÷10	20÷4	45÷9	35÷7	35÷7	50÷10	12÷6	18÷9	18÷9	12÷6
18÷9	4÷2	6÷3	4÷2	6÷3	6÷3	2÷1	10÷5	4÷2	16÷8	4÷2	21÷7	20÷5	9÷3	2÷1	4÷2	4÷2	8÷4	16÷8
2÷1	10÷5	8÷4	4÷2	4÷2	6÷3	2÷1	2÷1	18÷9	4÷2	20÷4	18÷6	3÷1	30÷10	30÷6	6÷3	10÷5	2÷1	12÷6
6÷3	10÷5	14÷7	16÷8	4÷2	4÷2	10÷5	4÷2	16÷8	12÷6	40÷8	6÷2	30÷10	24÷8	50÷10	18÷9	20÷10	14÷7	16÷8
2÷1	14÷7	14÷7	12÷6	16÷8	10÷5	20÷10	20÷10	10÷5	2÷1	15÷3	20÷4	21÷7	15÷3	5÷1	10÷5	4÷2	4÷2	2÷1
20÷10	21÷7	2÷1	9÷3	10÷5	18÷6	16÷8	9÷3	12÷6	16÷8	10÷5	16÷4	3÷1	24÷6	2÷1	8÷4	6÷3	8÷4	20÷10
8÷4	24÷6	35÷7	32÷8	12÷6	32÷8	40÷8	36÷9	4÷2	8÷4	4÷2	12÷4	21÷7	6÷2	10÷5	8÷4	12÷6	20÷10	4÷2
18÷9	25÷5	16÷4	45÷9	16÷8	10÷2	20÷5	30÷6	2÷1	18÷9	18÷9	18÷6	30÷10	30÷10	10÷5	20÷10	8÷4	20÷10	10÷5
2÷1	4÷2	6÷2	2÷1	4÷2	2÷1	3÷1	16÷8	18÷9	2÷1	20÷4	15÷5	6÷2	30÷10	20÷4	6÷3	20÷10	10÷5	14÷7
10÷5	35÷7	21÷7	50÷10	2÷1	35÷7	21÷7	40÷8	16÷8	35÷7	10÷2	18÷6	30÷10	27÷9	50÷10	35÷7	12÷6	2÷1	2÷1
2÷1	28÷7	27÷9	32÷8	4÷2	28÷7	27÷9	32÷8	8÷4	40÷8	35÷7	15÷5	30÷10	21÷7	40÷8	50÷10	20÷10	14÷7	2÷1
10÷5	30÷6	24÷8	20÷4	12÷6	30÷6	18÷6	10÷2	6÷3	15÷3	20÷4	3÷1	24÷8	9÷3	15÷3	15÷3	18÷9	18÷9	4÷2
20÷10	16÷4	21÷7	16÷4	18÷9	28÷7	15÷5	12÷3	2÷1	16÷4	32÷8	9÷3	3÷1	9÷3	4÷1	36÷9	6÷2	2÷1	12÷6
50÷10	35÷7	30÷6	30÷6	30÷6	20÷4	15÷3	20÷4	30÷6	40÷8	45÷9	15÷3	20÷4	10÷2	5÷1	45÷9	5÷1	35÷7	45÷9
45÷9	5÷1	40÷8	40÷8	15÷3	10÷2	35÷7	40÷8	25÷5	20÷4	45÷9	25÷5	50÷10	10÷2	35÷7	10÷2	25÷5	25÷5	35÷7

ANSWER KEY

We hope you learned a ton with this book, but most importantly we hope you had fun at the same time!

We love trees, so we've gone digital with our answer key!

 SCAN ME

OR VISIT:

uppercase "i"

https://bit.ly/3PIu1C0